Myth
or
Mystery?

Contents

Monsters of the Deep:
The Monster of Lake Iliamna   5

Monsters of the Land:
The Bigfoot File   14

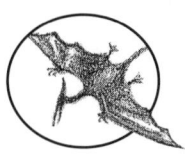

Monsters of the Sky:
The Search for Kongamato   32

Myth or Mystery?   43

Monsters of the Deep

The Monster of Lake Iliamna

A traditional Athabascan legend from Alaska

Long ago, in a land far to the north, a father, mother, and son lived beside a lake so large it seemed to flow into the sky.

The small family lived happily in their home by the lake. The father caught moose, caribou, and fish. There was also small game and, in the summer, there were berries of all kinds. As the son grew into a strong hunter, the father and mother felt they had everything they could ever want.

Life was good until one spring day – when the snows stopped and the wind was still – a great tragedy befell the family. The son went out on the lake, hunting caribou that were in the water hiding from hungry mosquitoes.

A caribou was soon felled, but as the son lifted the animal into his canoe, the lake waters began to froth wildly. Dropping the caribou, the son tried to paddle away. Suddenly, his canoe was sucked into the deep waters, and he disappeared from sight.

Although the father and mother searched and searched for their son, they never saw him again. They knew he had been captured by the fish monster that lived in the lake.

The father vowed, there and then, to kill the monster. All summer and autumn, the father cut down trees surrounding the huge lake. And that winter, he pushed all the felled trees onto the frozen lake.

There were so many trees that they covered the lake like a heavy blanket.

When spring finally came and the ice melted, the father set fire to the floating trees. After four days, the huge lake started to steam. After eight days, it began to boil. Suddenly, a sound like thunder split the air. In the waters below the place where the father and mother waited, the burning trees started to move. A giant snake-like fish, bigger than a massive herd of one hundred caribou, hurled itself out of the water and onto the barren beach.

The father had vowed to kill the fish monster that had taken his son, and he had done it.

Or Had He?

People who live around Lake Iliamna, the largest lake in Alaska, still see enormous snake-like shapes swimming in the lake.

Some think the "Iliamna monster" is really a herd of seals, or a giant fish called a sturgeon. The problem is that sturgeons don't match the description of what has been seen. While sturgeons can be more than 6-metres long, they swim only in the deepest parts of the lake – not near the surface.

Lake Iliamna does seem like the perfect hiding place for a monster. If a monster lives there, maybe it thinks so, too.

Monsters of the Land

The Bigfoot File

"...and when the family looked out of the window of their cabin to see what their dog was barking at, they saw a big, hairy creature running into the forest."

"Well, Kathy, it looks like Bigfoot is on the loose again – or, should I say, the Bigfoot myth is on the loose again?" the newsreader chuckled.

Daisy turned off the television and went out to the kitchen. "Grandad! There was a strange story on the news about a monster running about in the mountains!" she said with a laugh. "Are we supposed to believe it? Do they think we're silly?"

"Oh, Daisy, I wouldn't laugh about that news report if I were you. Bigfoot doesn't come out often, but many of the people who live around here are pretty sure he's real," Grandad said.

Daisy frowned. Her week at her grandparents' cabin in the woods of northern Oregon had just begun, and Grandad was already teasing her. Before she could complain, Grandad got up and pulled a dust-covered shoebox out of a cupboard. He smiled and said, "I have something to show you. Could you help me sort this out?"

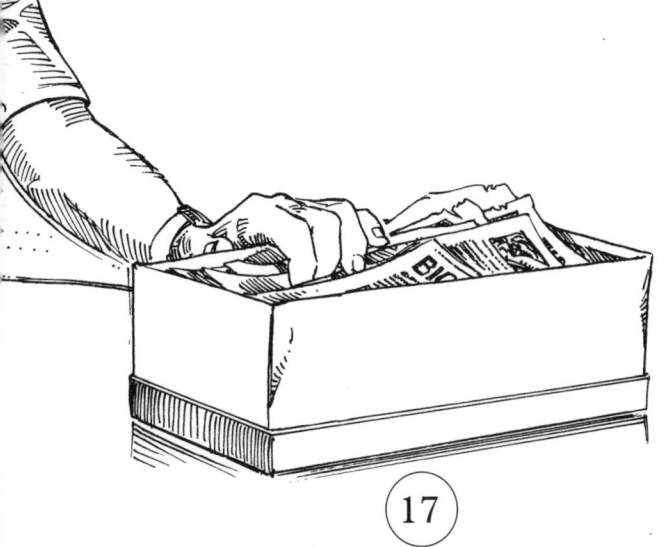

As he lifted the top off the box, a mountain of newspaper clippings and photographs came spilling out. On top was a yellowed article with a big, bold headline:

Bigfoot Sighted?

BRITISH COLUMBIA. A train driver and crew completely long black h

"Grandad, what are all these clippings?" Daisy asked, as she started flipping through the articles.

"Oh, just some records of local sightings of our furry friend. Your great-grandfather started this file in the 1920s when he was prospecting for gold in these mountains. I've been adding to it ever since he gave it to me."

Bigfoot Sighted?

BRITISH COLUMBIA. A train driver and crew encountered a strange creature during their weekly train trip.

The driver, thinking at first it was a man, blew the whistle in warning and brought the train to a squealing stop. The "man" jumped up, made a barking sound, and began to climb the steep, rocky hillside.

The crew estimated that the creature was about 140-centimetres tall and weighed about 60 kilograms. It looked like a man except that its entire body was completely covered with long black hair.

The "monster" – a hairy, gorilla-like animal – was last seen running along the rocky hills near the tracks.

Daisy was finding the whole thing very hard to believe. She held up one article titled "Why Did the Bigfoot Cross the Road?"

"Grandad, I don't understand," Daisy said. "If all of these people think that they've seen this Bigfoot, why doesn't the rest of the world know about it?"

Why Did the Bigfoot Cross the Road?

CALIFORNIA. A local couple was startled while driving in the mountains last night, when a tall figure crossing the road was caught in the beam of their car's headlights.

Asking her husband to slow down so that she could get a better look, the woman first thought the figure was a very tall person wearing a full-length fur coat. She believes the figure was nearly 3-metres tall, and seemed to be completely covered with short black hair.

"It was so strange. It had a big pointy head," the woman said. "It turned around slowly, and looked into our car!"

The couple doubts that what they saw was simply a man playing a trick. "Let me tell you, this furry thing was a lot bigger than any normal person," the man said. "Anyway, I can't imagine why anyone would want to dress up in a gorilla costume and walk across a road at midnight."

Local park rangers are investigating the sighting. One suggestion is that it could have been a bear, while others insist that a bear would never walk across a road upright on its hind feet.

"Well, Daisy, I think more people know about this than you'd think. There are reports of creatures like these in Australia, South America, Africa, Japan, and other parts of Asia. Somewhere here, I have some stories from an old Nootka Indian who used to live near by. I wrote down the stories as he told them to me. His tribe had countless legends about the local 'wild men' that they call Sasquatch."

"But isn't there any real proof? What about skeletons? How can people believe all this if they've never found any evidence like that?" asked Daisy.

"Well, when you think about it, that makes sense, too. Because of natural scavengers, people rarely find skeletons of, say, black bears, and we know that they exist. Some people think Bigfoot is related to humans. So, perhaps, it would bury its dead," said Grandad.

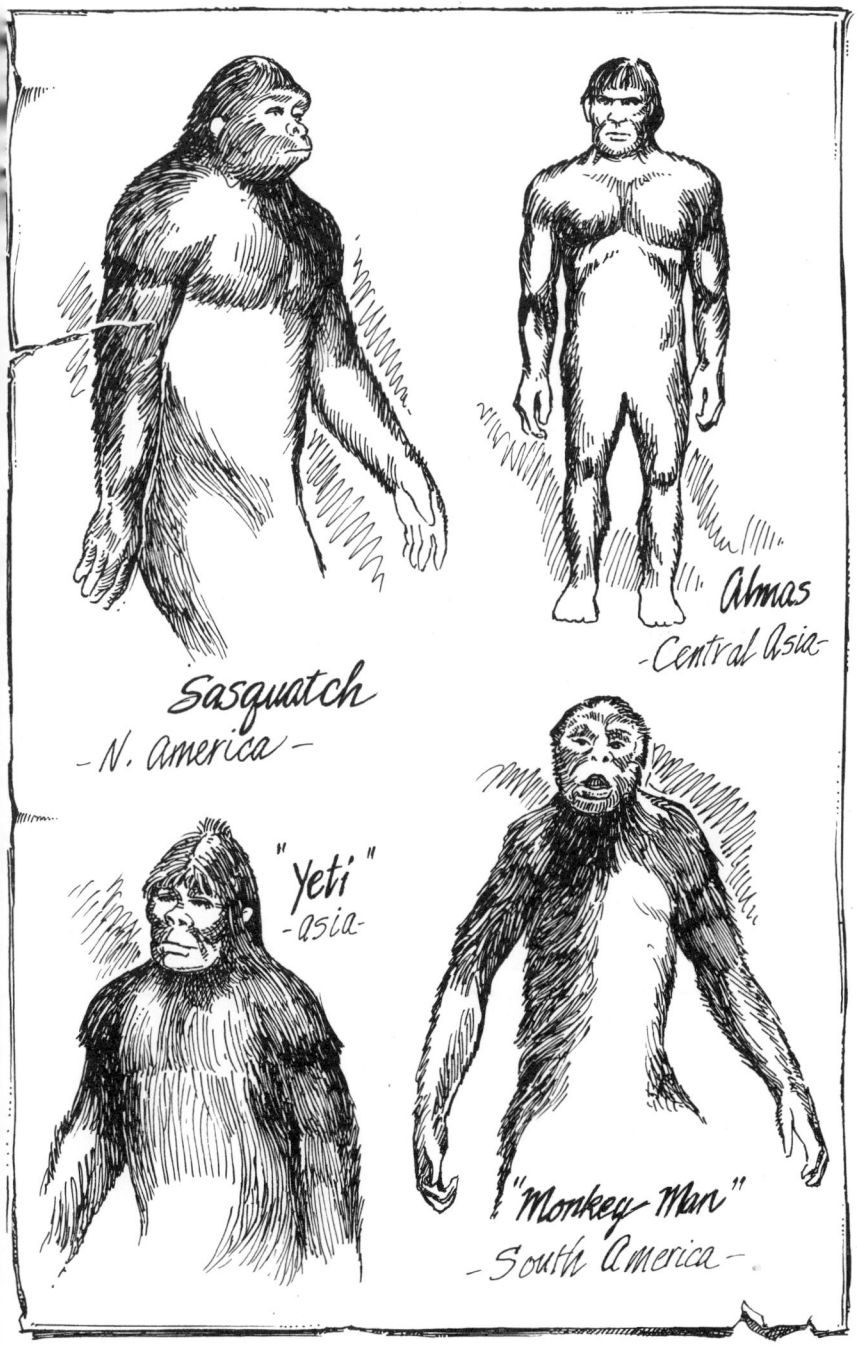

"Grandad, you sound as though you believe all this. Don't tell me you've seen one," Daisy said.

Without saying a word, Grandad pulled out an article, smoothed it out, and handed it to her. Daisy started to read.

Proof? Forestry Workers Find Giant Footprints

OREGON. A team of forestry workers may have found proof that Sasquatch is still roaming the hills west of Portland.

One of the workers first saw a number of huge footprints near his truck a month ago. The tracks lead out of the forest, and circled the area where the machinery is kept.

When the workers found more of the enormous footprints this week, they photographed them and also made plaster casts of the prints.

Scientists who are examining the evidence say that the footprints appear to have been made by a foot that is 41-centimetres long and 15-centimetres wide. The depth of the prints suggests that they were made by something that weighs well over 230 kilograms.

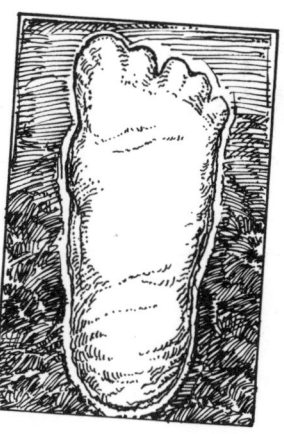

Daisy finished the article and looked up at her grandfather. "That sounds like they really did see something, but how do you know those prints weren't a trick?"

Grandad gave her a serious look, and then he said, "I know they weren't a trick, because I was one of the forestry workers. Some people get a kick out of wearing gorilla costumes and parading around in the woods, or making tracks to get attention, but I don't think that happened that time."

"Weren't you scared? I don't think I'd like the idea of staying here if I thought that some sort of huge animal was running around outside," Daisy said. "Some of these stories make this creature sound pretty mean." She pointed to a very old, faded article titled "Monster Ape Attacks Miners".

Monster Ape Attacks Miners

MT ST HELENS, WA. Four miners were attacked at their mining claim in a gorge near Mount Saint Helens. The workers had seen enormous footprints near their camp several times before, but they had never felt that they were in any danger.

Then, while eating his lunch two days ago, one of the miners saw a tall, hairy creature walk along a path high above the gorge. The miner fired three shots to scare the creature away from the area.

That night, the men were awakened by a loud thumping noise. They discovered that stones were hitting the roof and walls of their hut.

When the men went outside to find out who (or what) was throwing the stones, the stone-throwing stopped. However, it began again once the men went back inside.

The next night, it happened again. And last night, as the stones continued to rain down on the hut, the frightened men packed up their belongings and left.

Today, a search party that went into the gorge found huge stones lying around the little hut. The inside of the hut had been torn to shreds.

"Not really," Grandad said. "Most of the stories are about how gentle and shy Bigfoot is. I don't think that miner should have been firing a gun and trying to frighten whatever it was he saw. I don't blame the Sasquatch for throwing stones at the hut and wrecking the inside!" Then, he picked up a photo of his old hunting dog and smiled.

"Look, it's Austin! Why is his picture in the box, Grandad?"

"Well, once, many years ago, Austin was missing for over a week. I was sure something terrible had happened to him. Then early one morning, I heard something whining outside the door. I looked outside and there was Austin, lying on the back porch. His leg was mangled, and it looked as though he had been caught in some sort of animal trap."

Grandad took off his glasses and rubbed his eyes. "I was so glad to see him, that it took me a few minutes to notice he had some big leaves wrapped around his injured leg. It looked as though someone had given him first aid. He certainly couldn't have walked in that condition. Something, or someone, had rescued my dog and brought him home."

"So, you think it was Bigfoot?" Daisy asked.

"Well, I'll never know…"

The Search for Kongamato

June 3

I can't believe it – I'm finally in Africa, and tomorrow I start on my search for an animal that many people believe died out over 65 million years ago. I've read everything I can get my hands on about these bird monsters, and even if I don't find a modern-day flying monster, I think there must be something out there. Many people say they have seen it. Too many tribes have stories about it. Too many people believe it's true. I will check my list once more, and then it's off to bed. Tomorrow will be a long day.

June 8

We've been travelling through north-western Zambia for four days now and have left the cities far behind. We are entering the lands of the Kaonde, who are a tribal people with a folklore rich in stories of the bird monsters they call the Kongamato. Today, my guides introduced me to a tribe member who says he has seen this creature. He described a giant, bloodthirsty bird that looks like a lizard and has wings like a huge bat.

I showed him many pictures of known animals, but he just shook his head. Then, when I pulled out a picture of a pterodactyl — a prehistoric flying animal — he became excited and insisted that that was the creature he had seen.

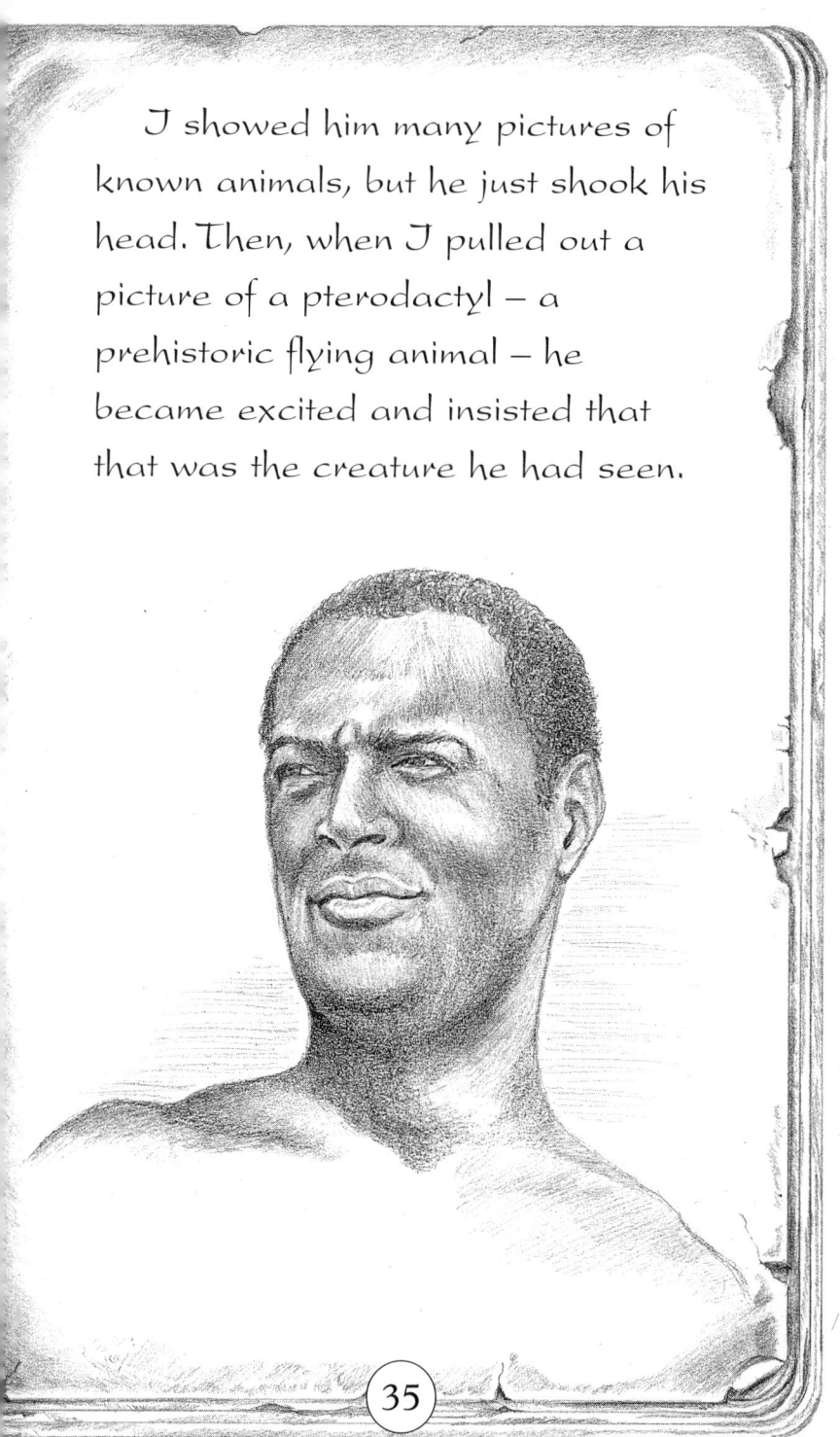

June 12

It's difficult to find an animal that leaves no trace except the stories from people who have seen it. Because of this, I've decided to look deep into the past to try to get an idea of what sort of life the bird monsters would lead, today.

If the bird monsters really are pterodactyls, we're looking for a species that supposedly became extinct 65 million years ago, and has a wingspan ranging from 10 to 12 metres!

Because pterodactyls fed on fish, lizards, and other small vertebrates, our best bet is to stay close to the waterways, where there is an abundance of this kind of prey. I hope my theory works, for I would love to find out, once and for all, what is behind all of these stories.

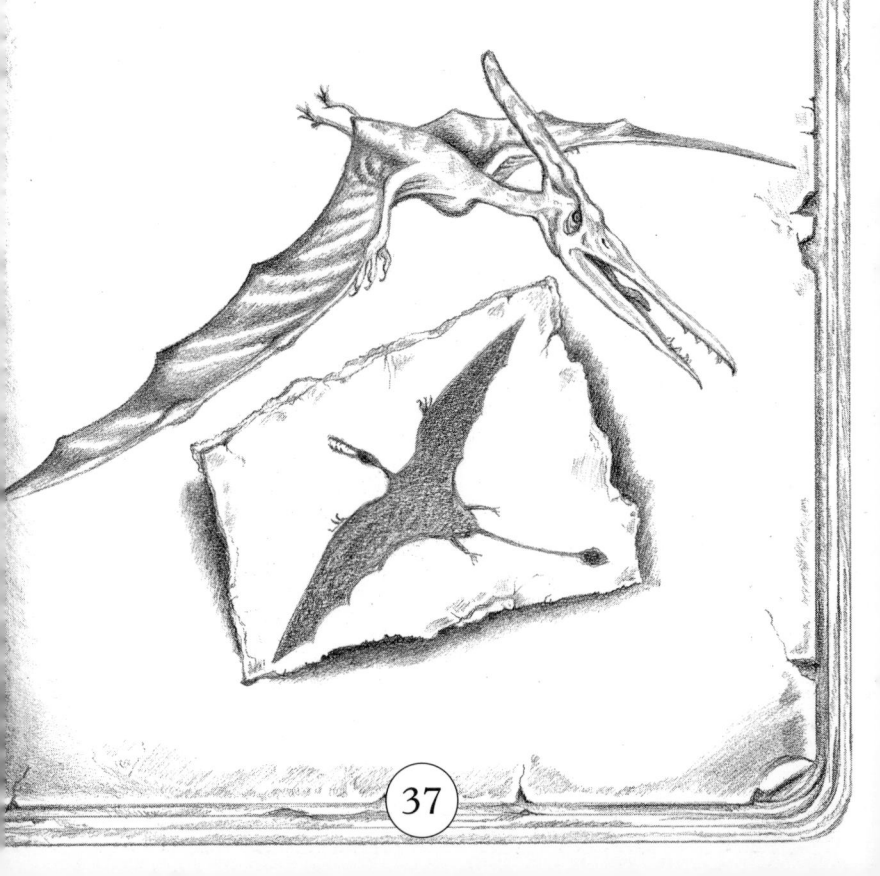

June 13

It is strange how the more things seem to change, the more they stay the same. Tonight, while we were sitting around the fire, I started swapping stories with my guides.

I told them about the legendary bird monsters from home. I described how Native Americans, who used to live along the banks of the Mississippi River, believed in the terrible Piasa bird. They carved and painted enormous pictures of the bird on cliffs along the river.

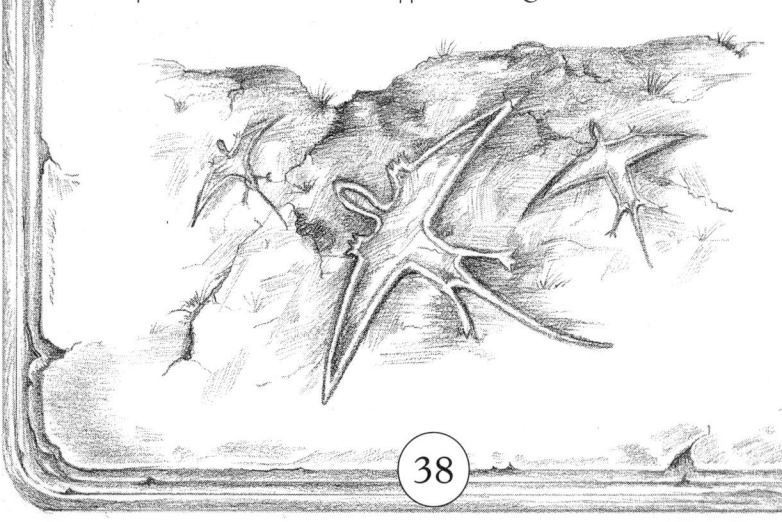

When I told my guides that the Native Americans believed the Piasa bird captured and carried away humans to feed its young, the guides nodded seriously. They said this bird monster sounded very much like their Kongamato. It seems strange that two completely different cultures, that live so far apart, should have stories of such similar creatures.

June 16

I am still shaking from what happened to me earlier today. What makes it even worse is that I think I may have missed my one and only chance to learn about the bird monster.

This afternoon, when we were preparing to climb a small butte that stood in our path on the way to the next river, my guides suddenly became very nervous and began chanting softly under their breath.

When I asked what was wrong, they said that the Kongamato was very close.

They were so afraid, that they refused to leave the safety of the jungle to climb up on the exposed rocks. I continued on my way, hoping they would eventually follow me to our next camp.

I had just reached the top of the rocky climb when it happened. Everything seemed to be fine, when I suddenly heard a tremendous swooshing sound. I was just turning around to see what all the commotion was about, when I heard a loud scream. The next thing I knew, something very hard and sharp hit the back of my head.

That's the last thing I remember. The next thing I knew, my guides were pulling me off the exposed rocks, and down to the shelter of the jungle undergrowth.

My guides tell me that I was attacked by the Kongamato, but as I didn't see what it was, or what actually happened, I can't be sure. In spite of my sore head, I'll continue my search tomorrow...

Myth or Mystery?

The Unicorn

Long ago, many people believed in this mythical animal, which looks like a white horse with blue eyes and a single horn coming from its forehead. The unicorn's horn was thought to have magical powers. Nobles often paid high prices for what they believed to be unicorn horns. In many fantasy stories today, the unicorn is still popular.

The Loch Ness Monster

For hundreds of years, people have told strange stories of an enormous, serpent-like monster that lives in a deep lake – Loch Ness – in the Scottish Highlands. There are more than 4,000 reported sightings of this monster, and even a few photographs. However, no one has really discovered what it is that lives in the lake.

The Lusca

Bahama Islanders tell terrifying tales of the Lusca – a giant sea creature that is half giant squid and half giant octopus. The Lusca is said to pull boats to the bottom of the ocean, and to leave huge round welts from its suckers on those who are lucky enough to escape its grasp.

From the Author

Many years ago, my grandmother used to take me to see pictures of the terrifying Piasa bird that were carved in the cliffs above the Mississippi River. Even though these carvings are now gone, my memories of them are still vivid. I get the shivers when I imagine strange, monstrous animals living in our midst.

While I've never seen any of the monsters mentioned in this book, my friends tell me that I live with two of the worst monsters ever – my two dogs, Basil and Stella!

Rebecca Weber

From the Illustrators

I have just moved to Denver from Chicago. *Myth or Mystery?* is my twentieth children's book. I like illustrating for children because it reminds me of what a great time I had drawing as a child.

Sam Thiewes

I live in Colorado with my children, Paul and Nicolle. I would like to thank Roland Booth and Megan, Matt and Rebecca Anderson for their help in illustrating this book.

Shawn Shea

I had a lot of fun illustrating my section of *Myth or Mystery?* I wondered what might happen next to the monsters or the people looking for them. I suppose that's a mystery, too!

Connie Marshall

ANOTHER TIME, ANOTHER PLACE
Cloudcatcher
Flags
The Dinosaur Connection
Myth or Mystery?
Where Did the Maya Go?
The Journal: Dear Future II

SOMETHING STRANGE
My Father the Mad Professor
A Theft in Time: Timedetectors II
CD and the Giant Cat
Chocolate!
White Elephants and Yellow Jackets
Dream Boats

CONFIDENCE AND COURAGE
Imagine this, James Robert
Follow That Spy!
Who Will Look Out for Danny?
Fuzz and the Glass Eye
Bald Eagles
Cottle Street

WHEN THINGS GO WRONG
The Long Walk Home
The Trouble with Patrick
The Kids from Quiller's Bend
Laughter is the Best Medicine
Wild Horses
The Sunday Horse

Myth or Mystery?

ISBN 13: 978-1-57-257747-3
ISBN 10: 1-57-257747-9

McGraw Hill Kingscourt

Published by:
McGraw-Hill Education
Shoppenhangers Road, Maidenhead, Berkshire, England, SL6 2QL
Telephone: 44 (0) 1628 502730
Fax: 44 (0) 1628 635895
Website: www.kingscourt.co.uk
Website: www.mcgraw-hill.co.uk

Written by **Rebecca Weber**
Illustrated by **Sam Thiewes** ("The Monster of Lake Iliamna"); **Shawn Shea** ("The Bigfoot File") **and Connie Marshall** ("In Search of Kongomato")
Edited by **Jennifer Waters**
Designed by **Mary C. Walker**

Original Edition © 1997 Shortlands Publications Inc.
English Reprint Edition © 2010 McGraw Hill Publishing Company

All rights reserved.

Printed in China by CTPS Limited

The *McGraw-Hill* Companies